23. 6. 23,

SHIP OF THE LINE

Penny Boxall was born in 1987. Her debut collection of poetry, *Ship of the Line*, was first published in 2014 and relaunched in a new edition by Valley Press in 2018, alongside her second collection *Who Goes There?*

She won the 2016 Edwin Morgan Poetry Award and the Elmet Trust Competition, and holds an MA with distinction in Creative Writing (Poetry) from UEA. In 2017, she became writer-in-residence at Gladstone's Library in Flintshire and a Hawthornden Fellow.

*by the same author*

WHO GOES THERE?

# Ship of the Line

PENNY BOXALL

*Valley Press*

First published in 2014 by Eyewear Publishing Ltd

This edition first published in 2018 by Valley Press
Woodend, The Crescent, Scarborough, YO11 2PW
www.valleypressuk.com

Second edition, first printing (August 2018)

ISBN 978-1-912436-05-7
Cat. no. VP0125

A CIP record for this book is available from the British Library.

Cover and text design by Jamie McGarry.

Printed and bound in the EU by Pulsio, Paris.

# Contents

# Taxidermy Outpost

We drive past the sign at first,
swerve, spin back.
                    It's hung
with skin, the crown of some
wrecked animal topping it all.
            They sell scented candles
and the recent dead –
a baby bear sits on a stool
            as if for a lesson,
his giant paw missing nothing
but a crayon.
            There's a pornographic hush
towards the back, the pelts
strung in moneyed lines,
shining like polished wood.
Leopards maul the walls.
            And a fawn/not fawn,
hauled from its mother,
is frozen in a pose it never struck,
its eyes filmy.
                    Outside is the Wild
which we only know about
because we know too of outposts
filled with fur. And look:
            here is a chipmunk
paddling a canoe, his little fist
just like yours.

# Williams, Who Lived

When this man was hauled from the foam
and, shaking, asked his name, the news spread fast.
They skimmed him back to shore –
a talisman, breaking the waves like eggs.

Hugh Williams had lived before. The name
confounded shipwrecks, made men float
through salted depths towards the aching
light. Williams was a lonely but a living sort.

It seemed the surest way to last gulp air not water,
to die dry, was to be him; or if not him
another of his kind. The parish registrars
scrawled Williams upon Williams as though they kept

forgetting. Williams married Susan, married
Mary, married Anne; and when he died,
(and died – and died –) the headstones
read the same, like yesterday's paper.

Williams stayed at home and picked rocks
from the binary of ploughed earth.
Or travelled, wrote a book; did
or did not like onions; wet the bed.

And when he went to sea – as captain,
passenger, stowaway – he kept himself
to himself: threw the name around him,
vein-strung, tenuous as a caul.

# The Observer

He lives like a bird in a tall nest, an Escher creation
of high windows and matchstick stairs. He pushes
his telescopes out on the roof for taking the light.

He lives alone, the stars are so noisy.
He has seen things most people would not even
care about – they are too far and too untimely.

The Plough continues its allotted furrow
and Orion stands perennially fast.
He's the watcher of blips, of brevity,

and his eye is as quick as a comet.
The Observer shares his plot with the hospital
where nudes manifest at the windows.

He glosses over their magnified exposure and writes
notes of complaint to the orderlies.
His is a godly life, pressed between two maps

like glass slides – the old town, pleasantly abstracted
by his height; and its negative, described in stars
at once up close and very far away.

# Borderline

Who knows why they built it here:
some grand Victorian joke. We come in
by one country and leave by another.
Leave fireworks and booze at the door.

Even the name is ambivalent:
*The Haskell Free Library and Opera House*
suggests the aria shushed from the wings,
the book snapped theatrically shut.

A tickertape border bisects the lobby
like a sitcom set. The pen on that
side of the desk; the paper on this.
The practicalities! We lean without touching.

The stage is no better:
it's in one ear and out the other.
We speak our lines from different countries
and finish each others' sentences.

## II

It's not surprising that the thing
burnt down. Nothing personal:
a match not spent, an incendiary remark.
Dual-purpose means there's twice as much to burn.

Imagine the ungovernable explosions,
the slide of melting glass – the sparks
shot from either side
into the night they held in common.

The fire destroyed the lobby,
burned up the lines.
Neither party was responsible
when it came to claims.

# Pentimenti

The artist regrets, regrets on top of varnish,
        erases his old certainties with fresh paint.
He lays on new strokes that will surely flake
        and fail because they have no other thing
to cling to, but he can't bear the work as it is.
        In time the ghost of his intention will shine
through, his mistakes will find their way.
        The sudden trees will not successfully obscure
the lounging naked nymphs he planted there before.
        A baby's face will triumph through imposed fruit,
and the misjudged hand, lying in the woman's lap,
        will betray its excess fingers, given time.
There is no room for error. He must make
        his first try better than his last mistake.

# The Lytel Treatyse

*Here beginneth a lytel treatyse that sheweth how euery man and woman*
*ought to faste and absteyne them from flesshe – on ye wednesday*
(Westminster: W. de Worde)

His hunger upholds him. Through the stone-hard
hours he dreams of dinners years-gone:

gooseflesh dissolving from bone;
berries' slow explosions; the way gin slaps

the chops. Under the bench with the dogs
as a boy, handed bread hot as the breath

of god that burnt him but was fresh
as a baby – it brought tears wobbling to his eyes.

And apples, old and original, each bite
singeing the tongue: he swallowed

the seeds beloved to the end, hopeful
that an orchard might burst from his core.

He sinks into it, deep as a Friday fish
in the antediluvian sea. Even the roots

withdrawn from the wintering earth he loves:
their blindness and their advent.

So he makes this amendment. One day is enough
to understand lack, to keep us from losing it.

# What Came First

It was the first fine day.
Not even hot – just that the sky
had broken to show itself, modestly,
startlingly blue.
We watched through the high
classroom windows: a shuddering
of cloud and sky.
After break we filed down the lane
to the burn behind the village.
It was overgrown, dank with weed,
and the trunks were mossy, moist
to the touch. Someone called us –
held a bird's nest, complete with egg,
an almost-dome inside an O.
"Look, the bird has left the edge
so neat, as if it sliced it, somehow."
The teacher balanced it
and led us, ambassadors, back to school –
where we found the egg gone.
Emptied, the twigs and hair
were no more than a palm,

an open grasp like the one
which took mine one afternoon
and led me to the staffroom
when I cried for the end.
She handed me
a strawberry tart – said,
"He's in heaven now," not adding,
as I thought she would,
"if there is a heaven." I studied
the crown of berries,
their rich sauce, wondering
if I should eat it if I could not say for sure.

# The Old Magic

They've crept into the walls: oddments
placed by hand for some misplaced
and misremembered purpose. You're never far –
knock the chimney breast and feel
how it knocks back.
   Curled like a leather dog,
this shoe has heard three muffled centuries,
learning its language second-hand.
Dear shoe, withstander of flames,
wedged secretly in the stack:
the soot has fallen into you like rain.
   When twelve generations of rooks
made their nests above you, you shirked
those muddy twigs and sulked. The wind
has rushed you, alarming, more times
than you care to remember. Now,
dislodged by new hands, you are borne
into the magnified world. You are less
of a shoe now; more a soft, cupped palm,
full of something we don't think to see.

# Etiquette

August, and the air is thick with salt.
We walk the sticky avenues,
take comfort in the momentary shade.
Above the twisted-sinew roots cement
bulges. Crickets tune their strings.

The grid of streets means turning right again
will bring us back to the beginning – it's here
that four are grouped round something
on the grass. A skunk, perhaps, or else
exotic moth – the teenagers

are absorbed. A squirrel? It lies
fat as a pear, legs spoked as though
through gorging. The girl glances;
embarrassment clears her throat.
"I feel bad for it," she says,

"with a broken back." Of course:
her friend dangles the despatching mallet.
Seconds tick. They're waiting for our exit
at the corner, past the shielding trees.
All the way, I listen for a sound.

# The Advantage

At dusk the light weighs on us:
sticky, shot through. After dinner
we are paired for tennis:
my father, much the better, and me.

The night is aswarm: winged prehistoric things
insist on our faces, searching for a hold.
The trees share nothing of themselves,
lofty in their disassembled dark.

My serve has always lacked pizzazz:
the ball keeps falling short. My fault:
I bounce to the net and back, then lob
and he replies, his easy forehand stuttering

against mine. But now the ball
refuses, makes contact with some hard part
of the dark and drops, stunned. The difficulty
is a bat, colliding with our ball –

knocked off course. It's a slight mousey thing,
webbed where you least expect it: it bleats
in no way we understand. O, it mouths,
O and O and O, – and then it's up

and lifts again, its path not changed
but altered. No harm done: we scrub
the point, turn back to where we started.
Your advantage, we both seem to remember.

Above our game, small shapes busy
themselves, sometimes dipping in
to our continent of light.

# Snowflake Bentley

The idea of our marriage formed and dissolved,
      too quick to capture. I forget whose idea it was:
I can't recall your ever having been indoors.
      You were out all day, wet-mittened, working with your blue
hands in a blizzard, oblivious. You spent the year
      with your eye on the weather, the clouds bursting white

like unstitched pillows. We made our agreement
      in spring, the last flurry of winter over. You were absorbed
with those precisions you had missed in your transient
      collection, your catalogue of ice. No two
were ever the same, you said – and each year
      altered you as you absorbed them. What could I be

to you, the same no matter how you looked?
      Your tenderness for snow was dear, but
the habit of love-loss made you philosophic.
      Each night, your beauties gone to the dark,
you'd show me what you'd seen, the crisp
      sublime stars like the fractals of a quilt.

The morning brought you a gift of a storm
      and you were out like a shot.
You are a yeti-negative, dark and small,
      the blizzard shaking up around you
until you are an impression,
      only an idea holding you together.

# Discernment

I have never been to Norway:
never stood on the needle of jetty
and split the lake's quick skin
with an incisive flint. Forests,
sheltering in gloom, are alien to me;
I cannot say that I have hiked
through thick-sapped trees and broken
at the top to sun and air. Low mists
have never touched me.

I have been to Sweden, though,
which, I imagine, is much the same.

# The Mauritian Specimen

Down on the beach the man extends
a cracker, shuffles backwards carefully
towards to the sea. The fat bird is lured like a herring.

*

That biscuit is the strangest thing she's seen –
far better than her sweet sun-blasted fruit –
and she loves this ripe pink man, his tall strangeness
and his limbs that reach like trees. She steps off
the last grass-covered inch and sears
her brittle feet on the sand for love, will follow
to the end of the earth, where it turns wet.

*

She gnaws the cracker edges in the dark for weeks, a notion
she can't grasp. Her head burns and flakes in the salt air.

*

She is turned out in the light with a flamingo and three quail.
She blinks at the candied fruit the ladies bring,
tongues it, negotiates its smoothness like a globe.

# Grand Tour

       Ice overtakes the unpeopled rocks
and robs them of contour.

       The traveller draws a blind
against this scentless view.

       Where the road dwindles he'll step out,
dismantle the coach, and climb
       in the sedan's cushioned nest to the peak.

His sketchbook is filled with vast
       hellish scenes of rocks and nothing.

He takes his scenery
       like his coffee, at a sit.

# Three Hares

The church, mile-distant, is slow waking.
It smells of powder, candle-wax,
the thick white scent of hymnals.
In a high-webbed corner, shadow-lit,
a trinity of hares is sharing just three ears
between them. They run their ring of wood,
legs crooked to fit.

Cook is in the steaming kitchen; the heft
of knife on wood is echoed by the slabs.
Along the table's length, the stripped limbs
lie. Quail and partridge nudge
soft secrets to each other, flesh pimpled
in the hot cave. The cabbage simmers fondly
on the stove, breathes scalding breath
against small windows. They stream from views
of constant snow – of blank sky falling into
lines of furrowed earth ploughed black
as liquorice.

Three hares – bare, and waiting
for the pie – lie ear-to-ear, each listening
to the next one's thoughts. They dream
of furlong fields, of hedgerows dark
as ovens.

# St Giles, from a Window

Thursday, and they're ringing in the night –
the birdsong tenor of the bells
    is looped like a complex knot.
They're practising for when it counts.
    The blossoms shake their little
heads but mean assent. They are light
    as ash, and do not last as long.
Spring is compacted, thick and green.

    The church is a stolid stone
in four lanes of noise, unmoved.
    In old prints this is a wilderness,
the packhorses tramping the last
    weary half-mile to the gates.
This used to be a walk, the church its end.
    When I open my window I am closer
to all of it, I let it all in.

I never see the weddings, but I hear
    their effect. The bells shake
fit to burst, each one shouting out
    so that traffic almost stops. Unseen,
inside, it's finished, and the bells begin again.
    Only the timing changes,
the high bells lagging, clamouring against
    that heavy bass-note which is always right:

though each one has to think that it
    will sound out loudest, count the most.
Each one has to think it, or the whole
    thing will crumble like wet cake. *And oh,*
*but this time is the best time, this time is the best.*

# Otter Hole

Sag-bellied, hammocks of fur,
they curl in each other's
collarbones, plump with sleep.

They are almost little dogs,
and yet not dogs (their long
sad upper lips, their child's hands

balled on their tummies
and their feet, more than anything,
bootless). We eavesdrop through

this window on their burrow.
Our faces must be vast,
and still they snore – their dreams,

if they are dreaming, catching
in their throats.

# Two Ladies

*Two Ladies of the Cholmondeley Family, who were born the same day,
married the same day, and brought to Bed the same day.*

And they look like a halved egg:
the twin shells frilled at the edge,

their faces brimming with the secret
of a double yolk. Their duplicate

offspring goggle the stars, bound
by cloth and something like love,

straight-backed and habited as nuns.
They have a talent for recurrence –

they imprint their lacy images as though
I am their mother, their first audience.

I carry them to bed with me, a sober
double-vision. They lie flat and quiet.

Though they might look like cobras
dancing high on the pillows,

artful enough to swallow an egg
without cracking the shell,

there is woman beneath all this:
arms in the stiff folds of the sleeves,

babies in those swaddled cones;
within the bone-and-metal torsos

the heart, yolk-red, and tugging.
How is it done, this doubling?

From whose dark origin did the other
split? In the lightless gallery

they look from their window and see
my impression after I have gone.

# Common Use

*The Pitt Rivers Museum, Oxford*

Suspicion breeds in dark, forgotten corners:
observing superstition is, or might be, wise
when the totem's angry beak is at your back.
Its head is huge. Behind the backlit glass, thick arctic furs
look lived-in. Consider those who walked behind
these floating lanterns, lit corridors and ships with them
in foreign dark; their fingers felt slick heat.
These pipes once puffed tobacco; unknown lungs breathed smoke
in forests, tepees, stone-and-mortar huts.
Those guns poured powder, taking pops at men
who swung these shields, displayed in this next cabinet:
if they're of the right vintage. It's difficult to tell.

More certain is the reluctance that you feel
as the keeper of the cave, the museum guard,
approaches with electric lamp and sweeps light
over witchcraft in a drawer: a mole's foot cleaved
for luck; a tip of human tongue; and, at the back,
a century's mould on a hot cross bun.
Pocketed, it kept someone, presumably, in health.
Every house, he tells you, in this fine scholastic city
has a ledge to keep the witches perched.
You leave and buy a postcard, and wonder
if your house is well enough prepared.

# A Book of Fragments

I catalogued so many textiles I lost count.
Muddy offcuts, snippets that should by rights
have been forgotten – minutes taken at history's
dry meeting. Some were "lightly soiled",
a euphemism for the dung clinging
to their naked warp and weft. I learnt
how the collector derided his condition:
how he'd loved his garden, the Latin names
and roots; would much rather have tended
towards botany.

I had to live with them, to make
from them my own peculiar
patchwork: linen, flax,
plain weave, tabby, twill.
Now when I try to type *woman*
*woven* forms itself.

# Everything I Ate at Barton State Fair

Even as we parked, settling dustily
in line with other cars on thirsting grass,
the blooming-onion stall was in full sight.
I'd been told about the delicious thick fists

of them, the crisped skin, the saucepot
balanced in their glib hearts. I was sold
before I ever found one, and here they were,
exploded globes the size of two cupped hands.

Next a candy apple, ripe as the world,
watching with its glazed eye as we shared,
cracked it, exposing fizzing white.
I'd had these before, but never this red.

Was it maple then? We had, certainly,
whipped maple creamies, smooth as buttermilk,
and soft mouthfuls of maple candyfloss,
tree-sweet; but that may have been after

the strange curried eggs bought from the man
who looked like a bearded egg – who had told us
in the first place about blooming-onions.
"If you like these," he'd said, his grey beard

lolling to his waist, "you'll love bloomin' onions."
We'd stood in the Vermont barn, ogling possibilities.
Either way, we also had Hawaiian ice, and not
just one flavour – I had the sun and moon

of Georgia peach and green apple, and we sat
on benches, paint bubbled with old heat.
There were others, too – a sausage hot
with jalapeños, a rack of barbecue ribs –

but only so much I'm prepared to own.
There were other things at the fair.
We skirted the high hocks of oxen,
picked through the caged hens and rabbits,

and on the way back averted our eyes from
the blooming-onions, to keep the memory sweet.

## There are Bears in Montana

And knowing this, I will forego
lush mountains, forests, rivers, snow.

# Follies

We round the Brunel coast, in a train
crowded with bags and elbows. Tunnels gape
through mountains. Someone coughs. Now at sea:
the dank sand rises from the surf, the strain
of mergence evident in straggled tapes
of kelp. The plate-glass windows frame these

quick pictures: someone heaves a fishing line
above the red seawall; another breaks
the lace of foam to hunt for early shells.
We swing from shore to estuary: here, pines
point fingertips on rounded grass that lakes
of mist promote as islands. On one hill

a flat-faced folly, crenellated, sits;
a battled cottage, military-spiked.
Near the train, imbibed in a salt six-inch,
the ribcage of a ship rots darkly. Its
metal spent, the look is almost Viking –
just as that shed is a castle – at a pinch.

Rising to my stop, I catch a face
suspended in the window's blur of breath.
I recognise the coat; it always takes
a moment more to recognise myself.

# On With the Game

Already, as we walk fluorescent lengths
to take our bare-boned seats, the anthem's
blazing from the ceiling. We pause –
the hotdog men in flannel shirts
are glaring from the benches. We slide

below their sightline as the first shots
rattle end to end, and bulked-up hockey boys
with names like Aaron Handler,
Chase Fletcher, Ryan Frat, hunch gracefully
between two posts, their cocksure spurs

scraping the ice brittle. We're never sure
what's going on. Brief pressings
of faces against rinkside glass
don't clear up ambiguities; the thwack
of wood on wood clatters our thoughts

and someone's down – the medic,
hoisted by his elbow, skids across
and gets the young man up, or half-up.
Something's wrong around the ribs:
he can't unbend. They blare soft rock;

propel him, by the buttocks, to the door.
Once he's out, the music stops
abrupt as a light switch; and then
the crowd's up, yelling – someone scores –
though which side's which we couldn't say.

# Love Lesson

"When they mate, their tails are stuck,
and they have to stick together."

My childhood understanding
of how foxes bred was tenuous.

But for me they grappled
like damselflies, knotting

their weary ends together –
unhappy bookends to the miracle

of love. They linked
like a furred handshake,

bent in the painful shape of a heart.
They would have to choose well:

a pair mated for life, or until
one of them gave up the fight

and lay down, to be dragged
by its eternal spouse

from bush to bush, in search
of some nocturnal thing.

No wonder you could hear them
screaming over the lovelorn fields

at night. Or why, catching one
at midnight in the road, his tail

sifted the ground, curved
like a question.

# Unpacking my Grandfather

The jackets – all but his best – the slacks
and braces were displaced, one way
and another. The shirts were immaterial.

We used the old shot tweed
for lagging, a waxed coat for a play –
it stood for something we could name,

a useful byword anyone could catch.
The semaphore of his ties was sunk
with him, though in the shed his waders stand

absurdly upright, full with husks the squirrels
hid there, taking stock at the first frost.
The brogues are under a fence of coats, paired

in ready steps. Above them
his hat hangs like an afterthought,
as if he's wandered through the open

doors into the half-lit film of evening
and will be back for it, given time.
It's shaped to him, stained with a forgotten

weight of rain and curdled smoke.
Of all his things this is the last,
when even the shoes have broken

their step, upped and left. Even on
the hook it is firm, it is full to the brim.

# The Counted

I mistake them for gloves,
pegged to the fence
to signal their lost owners.
As we shift closer,

hedging, there are many:
a tally of themselves,
unmatched. They wave like
dark flags, little moles

with their hands still
rosary-wide –
strung by their skin
and their teeth. They range

like octaves on the wire,
their own obituaries.
Someone, counting,
racked up this abacus:

took stock of the work
of a day, and by it
measured his worth.

# Eadweard Muybridge

Settled for a bet, the question of the gallop's
not, now, problematic. Laid down flat,
the horse is caught in frames of stilted life;
its hooves are undisputed in mid-flight.
He's solved the bison, too: hard-headed charge
across the desert scree is trapped in inch
by inch of film.
                        And then the rest: the nude
young woman on the stairs is walking up
and down forever. I wonder what that proved.
In fact, those frames of life of Eadweard's own
are not what we'd expect: it seems as though
his breakdown of the facts to black and white
was merely photographic.
                              His wife's adulterer
sent a note to her to meet – was undone
when Muybridge paid a visit with a gun
"in answer to his question" (not disclosed).
Did he see the bullet's silver progress
in beads of light that flashed inside his eyes
in zoetrope succession?
                              – his mind met
the cinematic urge to dramatise,
to annotate with images of movement, pure
and simple. He read the legal symbols
and in court admitted homicide;
the judge pronounced it justified – acquitted
him. Old Muybridge left to find the West:
                                          we've
proof of it in running herds of bison,
moving still. They're evidence enough
that we can watch through gaps, and guess it right.

# St Mary's Abbey Gardens

Leaving the house late
I catch the call meant for you

and it expands, choking the line.
I respond how I think you would

then carry the cannonball of it
to you through the park.

# The Origin of Species

Waist-in, and there's nothing for it –
no more feints, no stalling, or I'm just
a sodden failure simpering in mud.

I forget it: the heart-held threat
of the current, the noisome textures
unwelcome between my toes. Better

to leave the ground entirely: kick off the too-
smooth weed, the spiteful rocks, and tilt.
My own arms catch me.
                              The first movement

is too quick, my head jagging like a pigeon,
legs flailing against the unknown quantity
that holds me. It's both easier and harder

than it looks. Sudden flashes of the toothed
things in the murk, their foreign eyes
periscoped, make me flurry. My pale distorted

legs must seem an inspiration to them.
          Slowing, sculling, the sky is bigger
from the water. Swallows dip to the brink,

after flies. The odd drop announces
the flick of a fish fly-catching. The two
meet halfway, pale reflections.

                              The sky is beginning
to drop: and overhead an air balloon
is drifting, fire-led. I can hear them

talk – far off, like ghosts. I tilt up, start
to walk through water to the shore –
wave a wet arm, knowing they won't see.

# The Mutineer Drowns

I

## William McCoy

From blind roots I tap my proof,
tug the muscled bulbs from underground
and shake them free of dirt, now birthed.

Their rude undersides swell like breasts
in the unseen earth, a dream in three dimensions
as un-akin to paper botany as bottle is to teat:

those flaccid still-lifes that the ships take back –
the careful hatchings, ink-and-paper clarity.
The tongue will only answer to the page

as far as mind allows: the folks at home
will look at that, see *pear* or *blackberry*;
the almost-weight of it in hand

since memory prescribes it,
not because the art is accurate.

## II

## MATTHEW QUINTAL

We baked the root to let the liquor out.
The nights I caught him blubbering neat tears
at the moonlit sea! I heard him choking,

gulping, choking, sighing one night
in the still grasses. I had the woman
by the hand and would have had her,

except for her pity; she coaxed him,
he cursing her through rotted teeth,
and put him to bed. Inherited women!

I would have had her – there
where the sweating fool depressed us –
had planned it so, but for him

and her pity. He made a mother
of my soft wife, for which
I bit her soft ear from her head.

III

## John Adams

Who was it found him? A woman
screaming, certainly, rushing horizons
over rocks to tell us where.

A stumble, it was generally agreed,
though she spoke with clarity
of rope-bound hands and feet.

I shouldn't like to say, but bury him
I did, the breeze turning pages
of my lost ship's Bible.

It is not for us to say.
History rewrites itself,
will right itself.

I saw the ship flaming,
with Quintal down below
making the choice for us

with his purging flame.
We made the choice for Quintal
with the bottle and a hatchet.

My children learn the language
from my Bible and from me:
*Thou shalt not* is relative.

It is hard to learn in negative –
it always begs the question.
I live this soft life of women

and children, the last man
in the world.

# Named Thursday October

## FLETCHER CHRISTIAN

His affliction was the taste of salt. No flavour
was simple: even a gentle fruit gone soft in the sun

was turned savoury. He'd always had the look of the sea:
wet prints on his sheets, the tide-mark on his leather boots.

He left a wake behind him so that he was easily
found. He spoiled things without meaning to:

his wife bore constant imprints of his palms.
But their son – a small unmoored thing,

born of a dry October – he marked with his name
and nothing else that spoke of English soil,

baptised him in the sweat of the father.
Water in water leaves no trace.

# The Breath and the Lord

NED YOUNG

They woke me after the fact:
I'd snored through the revolution,
dead to the tilt in the ship.
I sided with the way it rolled.

They baptised me in salt-water
like a fish, but oh my heart
bit at that line and tugged,
hauled gasping to the Light.

Once in a travelling show I saw
six angels engraved on the head
of a pin: not one more
could be crammed in.

Now we are two. I map
our blue circumference
with a dark-fuelled pin,
turn ink to flesh.

Above this sign I mark my heart
at cross-purpose, raw
with salvation. My breath
is shallow, it snags the air.

One day my lungs will rend
and beach. Till then, I love
each brimful as I take it:
shout out loud so I can hear it.

# The Flood

The roses, diluvial, drop their scent. Quickly
I dive between the showers into the warm
pool, swimming loose circles like dropped leaves.

I float. In the middle I collide with a tiny unmapped
island: a bee breaching the water's gathered skin.
I have heard that the pollen is flooded away, cutting

bee-life in two like the plan of some half-baked,
mad old Noah. But I am mindful not
to get stung, and in avoiding contact knock it

unhelpfully underwater, its little brown
self suspended farcically out of its element.
Eventually I pluck up a green leaf, and scoop,

delivering its no-weight back to the world.
Over and over it wrings itself, shakes, pokes out
its furred proboscis, combs and spits. I watch its wings

unstick from its back and its mortified
shuffling dance, waiting for it to recognise
salvation and take off. Still it shivers, long after

the wings have reworked their subtle magic
and everything's in place. It turns on the spot,
not finding up, until finally I turn too, leaving

it to its spent dignity like the woman in the home
who, like this, would not stop dancing.

# The Port Meadow Wedding

*for Sarah and Rob*

Here you can trace the undug archaeology –
horses, none the wiser, follow the line of a lost racecourse.

A pile of soil will overturn a pharmacy of bottles;
drained of medicine, they're as true and intact
as they were in the past. Badgers unearth them
in the dark like apothecaries.

The Isis brims with ancient fish.
They punctuate the surface in unbroken code.

Upstream, the nunnery presents its foundations,
has no need of a roof. It holds the strength
of the day in its walls, and all night smells of the sun.
The new leaves ache and stretch; and the whole
of the summer is still promised, yet to come.

The moon wobbles into the air,
big and certain with the light it's kept to itself
all this time, to share it now.

# Grandma and the Bomb

One day she cycled through
    the raindrop spread of an explosion,
        its magnetic circles hitting her
          like waves.

            The street did not take sides;
        but, besotted with the bomb,
      her hairpins leapt towards it.
    Even at that distance the blast
would take this from her.

# Halfway Up an Elephant

Johnny and Jane had done it: scaled the eight feet or so
to the summit of a fibreglass elephant, using the ladder
sunk into its ribs. They were up with the benefit
of height, surveying from their better vantage
the peculiar real-time map of where we'd been,
fairytale creatures dotted about with surreal props:
a misshapen leopard you could ride on;
the three bears' secretive hut; two little pigs on standby
beside their tumbledown shacks and the third smug
with his bricks and planning permission.
                              Halfway up an elephant felt unsafe
but I couldn't budge up nor down.
I'd longed for new perspective and had achieved only
an elephant's middle, its flank and treacherous rungs,
my field of vision compacted to a small weathered square.
Once Dad had noticed he tried to unpick me
from the grey limbo I'd made for myself, neither here
nor there. It took some doing, my hands gripped so tight:
for all the world as if I wanted to stay halfway up an elephant,
my breath recycling from her cold side back on to me.

# The Laird's Lug

The Highland-granite walls are three feet thick.
The windows, shut against the gritty wind,
still squint at lonely plains of castle lawn.
Here, high as a beanstalk, we strain to hear
full-bellied lowing from a hidden herd,
or muffled shufflings from a floor below.

In halls above the frigid gallery,
we traipse past portraits of the olden dead;
through libraries of the books they would have read,
or maybe did not read. (The vellum Histories
look dry as dust.) In a squat white room
of undetermined age, a corner holds

an unexpected hiding place: a chink
of light betrays a time-old paranoia.
A wooden step leads into whitewashed hush,
a trapdoor in the boards; and – the mystery –
a rough hole opens, undetected, through
the floor onto the gallery below.

The laird's lug, it is called. I think of him,
his knees bent to the rich dirt of the ground,
his ear pressed, anxious, to the gap, to learn
imagined secrecies, or otherwise:
perhaps to learn – much worse – of eavesdropped
mutiny; to crouch in wide-eyed dark.

# Penny-Farthing

Perched like a bird on a spun nest,
this is how to soar while sitting still.
You sense speed rather than feel it:
the crowd slipping as though
it was no big thing; the trees hanging
on and the iron rails zipping
in vertical flashes.
This is what it is
to be on top: both the giant
and needy Jack, high on his own
sprung apparatus. Spin past
the tilted hats in a blur
of concentrics – like the spread
of a raindrop in water, this is a trick
of near-misses.
Dismounting's another:
such pomp calls for an end
on a grand scale. Slide,
wobbling, to the zoo; befriend
a giraffe. Eat peanuts
by the monkey cage. Feel
how the firm ground shifts
with each footstep. The big
machine is chained to the gates,
useless without your slim propulsion;
though it is something to be god,
high and probably, therefore, mighty,
the world a wheel of secret orbits
whirring below and never touching.

# The Switch

There's an edge to every year.
For all the milk-ripe calves
there's still a small sad heap
that didn't make it, stopped

at the stage of flesh and bone.
Its mother bursts with milk
and stands lowing at the great gate
unanswered.
                    So that her labour
isn't wasted, her not-quite-calf
is flayed, its still-wet skin
lashed to a rejected calf – a twin
that has no hold on its own mother –

and brought to her to use her milk.
But the cow is old and will not be fooled.
She sniffs the known edges of the hide,
stops loving where the thing gets unfamiliar.

# Prudence in the Age of Steam

The country is dissected like a pie.
From tracks that never cool

the steam escapes: the funnels
are china blackbirds, open-mouthed.

Prudence mounts the steps.
The orbit of her hat

discourages her face.
The tunnels have strange currents.

She has heard of thefts, of hands pressed
in the dark, revealed by daylight

to be faces of the mild, the travel-blank.
The train slams into night.

She is ready with a pin
between her lips.

# The Wood for the Trees

The sea is full of splinters,
the rolling of a hundred decks
competing for a bloody horizontal.
This is not to mention the noise,

which you'll understand is monstrous –
like vast lungs filled with breakers.
A great mast, felled, rends the planks,
and the men are broken too,

though not so tidily. I was up there
when we got him, all the swaying masts
like a forest, so close, and us tight
in them. We were all firing at once,

popping a cloud of gunsmoke round us
so none could say for sure whose shot
it was that hit him. We'll each take
credit for it, those of us who live.

# The Journey Up

For years they perfected the bike –
whittled it down from its great heavy height
to this slim contraption, zooming down
towpaths or tethered to library gates.

In swift generations the light and fleet
left the blundering mammoths behind.
A simple idea, just the means to an end;
a slice of intent, its tyres thin as pennies.

It is hard to pretend it wasn't built just
for the fun of it, for going further
and more quickly than we should. For hefting
us uphill for the improper speed of the view –

and for casting off at the top of the hill
when we've got where we wanted,
the machines splayed happily in the grass
and us under the sky, solidly at rest.

# Coast to Coast

## BLAKEY RIDGE

The second night we are
moored in a drift, perched above
a monochrome valley in a pub built
by monks. The power out,
we eat pies in the half-dark, lit
by candles and the grate.

An hour earlier we'd sat in the village
in knackered twilight, scoffing our last fruit-and-nut
on a bench. The phone was dead in its booth.

Rewind the spool of the road:
feel how a mile can stretch like a worm, how
drifts collapse into monuments.
We were aiming for a little hut
that did not get closer, just slipped.

After three hours floundering
we came to, packed it in and plumped
for dependable tarmac:
the long way round, but gained
at least in miles instead of feet.

# EGTON

The day had started meekly:
breakfast in a mouldy Victorian room
which opened onto the clear morning.
The path rode the curve of the moors.
Sounds were curtailed, our voices
studio-precise. The snow had frozen
in arrested waves, each higher,
more ambitious, than the last.
        We startled the grouse from their nests.
They made an apocalypse noise
and flapped like little machines. We worried
for their hearts each time, running themselves stupid
for fear of us when we were just blundering by,
our pockets crammed with chocolate. But we were new
to each of them, every time a fresh disaster.


# INGLEBY CROSS

A day with a meniscus – the only sounds
are birds and water, and the sun

gives a nervy April light. We play
slow catchup with an old gent

hauling his bike uphill on foot
so he can whizz downhill on it like a king.

As we crest a little slope and overtake
he lifts the pipe from his mouth, salutes –

"Know where yur goin'?" – and hops on,
coasts out of sight. It is not really a question.

# Rush

Let me tell you about things I've seen:
midday men lined toe-to-heel in dust
ruts, creaking with the dirt, their hands
all bitten to the bone, their faces sunk,
all waiting, waiting; and the shift
from heat to sweating desert dusk

and then to particle-charged dusk
of underground. There's nothing to be seen
down there, but then you'll hear the shift
of falling silt, the settling of silver dust
through cracks in hidden stones, men sunk
under yards and yards of weight, their hands

metal-burnt. You should see their hands,
all red-raw, blistered in the campfire dusk.
We don't talk much to each other, sunk
in thought and aching. Things we've seen
by daylight are the same – the dust,
the heat, the sorry shrubs. Shift

work means we often come off shift
and see the next-day men, their hands
loose and off-guard, the skin of dust
not yet reached their faces. At dusk
we're ourselves caked. Have you seen
how thin a man can get, how sunk

into himself – the way his face is all sunk,
thin-skinned? I've watched them shift
from tanned lean daylight boys, seen
them turn to silver in the dark, their hands
pickaxed into shapes. But now, dusk
is on us, and you're thirsty from the dust

that's stuck in your throat. That dust
will catch your voice, take it, sunk
in layers of dirt. I'll see you at dusk,
friend, once your awaited shift
is ended. Let me look at your hands.
You're not the strongest I have seen.

# The Lovable Smee

*To tell poor Smee that they thought him lovable!*
*Hook itched to do it, but it seemed too brutal.*
(J.M. Barrie, *Peter and Wendy*)


Smee, who "stabbed without offence",
was darning on deck,
wielding the needle like a cutlass.

It shone in the light of the moon,
gathered to the mend
all the soft sounds of the night:

the water's slap
on planks, the slipping somewhere
of a creature out of mud –

the kidnapped breaths.
He asked a girl to mother him,
to hold his tyrant hand.

Had they locked him up
they would have wept at his plump hands
gentle on the bars.

# The King's Bed

Tradition holds that on a wet starless night
in 1665 the King slept in this bed, or one quite like it.

He lay his head, or might have, upon a facsimile
of this pillow. And in the morning, that probably

fresh pleasant morning in 1665 or thereabouts,
servants, in befitting manner, brought him the sort

of breakfast popular in those days, dressed him
in the garments that would have been the fashion.

What is known is that he was the monarch
living in those times, and so slept somewhere.

Nearby houses will make their own claims.
By reading this you have brought him to this bed.

# At Jorvik Viking Centre

The askance realism of the smell
is least convincing, once all is said and done.
Human sweat has never smelt like that.

Neither has a gutted fish, nor hearthfire.
I find imagination strongest in the dark
unpeopled nooks of hut and street, the fever-dream

of English playing through speakers. They're keen
to point out similarities: hear how *ugligr*
is ugly to all ears. Just as, I suppose,

that childish taunt of *ner-ner ner*
exists in every language, just the same:
provokes the same exasperated groan

and the same swipe around the head.
I draw the line at the fossilised turd
they've locked behind glass;

and at the splintered skeleton of a man
of around my own age, or so they tell me.
I can't quite see it, myself.

# Time Again

The light is failing. From unnumbered houses,
down the lanes, a ghostly monarchy
is having its succession: from the butcher's shop

come forth a king and queen who did not
go in. On the cobbler's steps, silk-bowed slippers
are newly heeled, and the baker's window

is a treasury of buns. The green
is a hunting ground bristling with hounds –
the cats take the part of the deer.

Jousters knock each other down
by turn, a Victorian politeness.
A bullfight is promised where appropriate.

The town has thought of everything – though
the tailoring is slightly out of true:
ladies are upheld with pins and tucks.

In the Royal Oak, warm with beer, an illicit
duke is harboured. On the hat-rack a cap
and coronet absolve each other.

Flotsam will be turning up for weeks –
buckles, silk rosettes, imperfect jewels.
The paper crowns will melt in the first proper rain.

# What You Mean to Me

You say your postcode slowly for the form,
an assertion of home and where you'll return.

I get the first half, then wait on you
like the bingo-caller, intent on a full house.

"I lived in Hill Street," I say, and we gawp
at each other, both of us miles away. "So do I!"

I meet your wife: we don't need names. We name
our numbers, like convicts. Mine had a red door

and a weed-matted garden. It is the same
now, you say, and we smile like old

fishermen, dragging it all back.
We hope for more coincidence

(my father once signed a cheque
for a man in a shop who said,

"But that's *my* name," like Dad
was somehow wearing it to a party,

stealing his best lines,
making his girlfriend laugh)

(and speaking of parties, my mother met
a woman at New Year who'd Christmassed

in the house we'd barely left,
with our carpets, our just-gone past)

but we don't know where to start.
You fumble with your wallet.

"What's your pin-number?" I want to ask,
in case we match again. For a year, innocent,

we'd shaped our no-shape lives
between the skimmed-milk walls, just feet

apart. *Who are you?* Please, identify.
*Can you tell me what you know of me?*

# Railway King

The Howsham houses lean their bricks in close
and talk amongst themselves. The bell shouts
from the ivy-creeping graveyard, makes known
its message of redemption – clears the air.
March ice is cracking on the ground.

Young George is not in church. Bonnets snap
to look behind, and blinker the view
of hymnals. George is not in church.
Hudson's there, his face obscured with his red
cloth-bound book; he's wearing something drab.

He sent a rider with the dawn,
a procurement of apprenticeship, made fast
with shilling notes. His son's to be a draper
in the city, after everything's patched up.
That girl cost money, too, a bundle

of the stuff. He'll have pride enough,
he speculates, once he's made his way.
But now, he's in a fix. Over
the fields, the ingenious young man
is running trouserless from town.

# A Balloon Flight

*for Jenny and Alex*

The morning is delighted with itself. My train
bites through the frost, the striped brown fields.
Sparrows carry themselves lightly,

little things, and blackbirds crack the code
of evaporating night. The sunlight alternates
with still-dark hedgerows, caught in waking,

and the moon is still in the cut sky,
shining her own silver difference.
The river edges by. In this stippled field

they are filling a balloon, the first of the day,
with a great lungful of that breaking air.
Spread like a rug on the hard earth, it shifts –

the red cloth catching like a brilliant idea –
and takes its shape; a globe, a great red heart
tethered to the comfortable, improbable basket,

which is foundation enough for those
standing on air. With height, the landscape
will become a map of itself, both known and new.

Now, you two have mapped yourselves together,
made of this strange world something familiar.
Your flight is ready, it is taking to the air.

# Navigavi

They sent my father's father to the desert.
He worked on aeroplanes and tanks,
a seed inside their boiling metal husks.
He tickled the wheeze of purpose
from the scrap while the world spun
with propellers.
      At night he lay on
the cold sand and by day he stood
on the hot sand.
      Once, a beetle,
seeing no other way, blundered
into his ear. It swam the tiny orbit
of his hammer and anvil, a waxy
navigation, and was amber-trapped
before either of them knew it.
      It had its genesis
in a hot human cave.
It bent to my grandfather's work
as he did, heard the bombers
guzzling like bees.
      When they sent for him
he carried it aboard, a tiny cargo.
In the canal of his ear
it kept its own horizon
while the sea brought his stomach
aching to his mouth.

Unknown, it was the mascot
of the man for years. He carried it
through the rain and it heard things meant
for him.
     It buzzed with his vow,
trembled in response; and buried
the keenness of my father's
baby-cry – if he slept on the good ear
he was untroubled.
     Strange, then, that he allowed
castor oil into his head.
It slipped past the hard stone
which someone whipped out
with a cotton bud.
     The new noise,
that first unhindered day,
was dumbfounding.
He couldn't miss a thing.
     But he kept the beetle –
if that is the word for
the rattling nut
hooked from his head –
in a jar. If you asked
it would say: *I have sailed.*

# Notes

'Williams, Who Lived': Three men – each named Hugh Williams – were the sole survivors of three separate shipwrecks in the seventeenth, eighteenth and nineteenth centuries.

'The Observer': This poem is set at the Radcliffe Observatory, Oxford.

'Snowflake Bentley': A pioneer of snowflake photomicrography, Wilson "Snowflake" Bentley was born in 1865 in Jericho, Vermont.

'The Mutineer Drowns', 'Named Thursday October', 'The Breath and the Lord': These poems are based on incidents from the lives of the *Bounty* mutineers. Fletcher Christian was known for sweating prodigiously; Ned Young had a talent for sleeping through anything, and died of asthma on Pitcairn Island.

'The Laird's Lug': That is, "The Lord's Ear", a sort of auditory "spyhole" in Castle Fraser, Aberdeenshire, through which the laird would listen to supposedly private conversations being held in the room below.

'The Wood for the Trees': This poem is set at the Battle of Trafalgar. The man who shot Nelson was himself shot moments later.

'Time Again': In 1885 Lord and Lady Wantage held a lavish Tudor-style pageant for the citizens of Wantage.

'Railway King': The railway financier George Hudson fathered a child at fifteen. He went on to become the "Railway King".

# Acknowledgements

Grateful acknowledgement is made to the editors of the following journals, magazines and anthologies in which some of these poems first appeared, some in an earlier form: *The Rialto*, *Mslexia*, *Tate Etc*, *The Oxonian Review*, *The Harlequin*, *The Salt Book of Younger Poets* (Salt), *Lung Jazz: Young British Poets for Oxfam* (Cinammon/Eyewear), *Cycle Lifestyle*, *Eight Poets* (UEA creative writing anthology, Egg Box Publishing) and competition/festival pamphlets for Live Canon, Segora and Poetry-Next-the-Sea. Thanks also to the judges who placed my poetry in the Frederick van Eeden, Museum of London, Segora, *Mslexia*, Live Canon and *The Oxonian Review* competitions. 'The Lytel Treatyse' was commissioned for the WEYA festival; 'Time Again' and 'The Old Magic' were written for the Oxfordshire Museum's *Head Over Heels* exhibition.

Many thanks to Andrew Forster, Michael Laskey and John Siddique for their kind endorsements; to Rebecca Watts for her cheerful and insightful editing suggestions; to Andrew Murray and Maureen Hopkinson for their encouragement; to Steph Wales for walks and exploring; to my friends; and very special thanks to my family.

I am hugely grateful to the judges of the 2016 Edwin Morgan Poetry Award, Jackie Kay and Stewart Conn, for awarding the prize to this book.